Christopher Columbus

Discover The Life Of An Explorer

Trish Kline

Rourke Publishing LLC
Vero Beach, Florida 32964

PHOTO CREDITS:
©Archive Photos: page 4; © James P. Rowan: page 12; ©Artville LLC: page 13
Library of Congress: cover, title page, pages 7, 9, 10, 15, 17, 18, 21

EDITORIAL SERVICES:
Pamela Schroeder

Library of Congress Cataloging-in-Publication Data

Kline, Trish.
    Christopher Columbus / Trish Kline.
        p. cm. — (Discover the life of an explorer)
    Includes bibliographical references and index.
    ISBN 1-58952-066-1
    1. Columbus, Christopher—Juvenile literature. 2.
Explorers—American—Biography—Juvenile literature. 3.
Explorers—Spain—Biography—Juvenile literature. 4. America—Discovery
and exploration—Spanish—Juvenile literature. [1. Columbus, Christopher. 2.
Explorers. 3. American—Discovery and exploration—Spanish.] I. Title.

E111 .K64 2001
970.01'5—dc21
                                 2001019000

Printed in the USA

TABLE OF CONTENTS

A BOY DREAMS OF THE SEA

Christopher Columbus was born in 1451. He lived in Italy. He was the oldest of five children. His father was a wool weaver. As a boy, Columbus learned to weave wool. His father wanted him to run the family business. However, Columbus had other plans! He wanted to be a sailor.

Columbus knew he would become a sailor.

ESCAPE FROM PIRATES

Columbus began to plan for his life upon the sea. He learned to read and make maps. When he was 14, Columbus got his first job on a ship. He was a ship's boy. He cleaned the ship. He helped the cook and the sailors.

Columbus went to sea at the age of 14.

Soon he was hired as a sailor. He made many **voyages**. On one voyage, his ship was attacked by pirates. The ship was burned. Columbus escaped by swimming to shore.

LEARNING ABOUT THE SEA

Columbus sailed many voyages. He learned more and more about map making. He studied books about **geography**. He learned about the wind and how to **navigate** a ship. He wanted to explore the oceans to the west. He went to many countries such as England, Iceland, and Ireland.

Columbus learned map making and studied geography.

Columbus was the first explorer to find the New World.

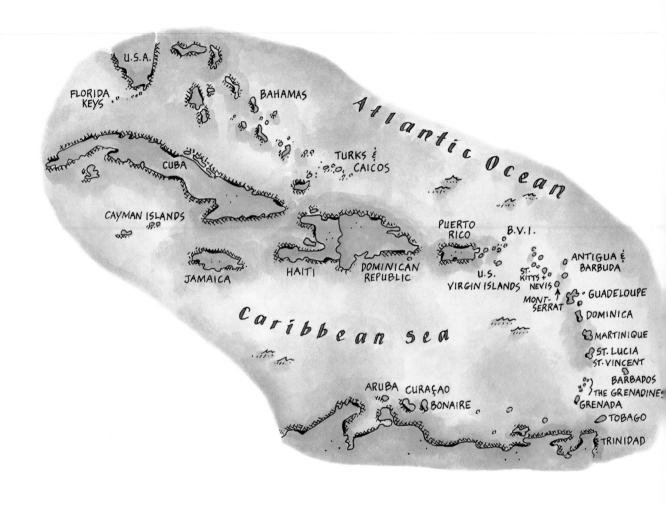

Columbus landed on an island in the Caribbean.

THE PLAN

Columbus believed that the world was round. Many people in his time thought that the world was flat. They thought that someone could fall off the edge of the Earth! Columbus drew up a plan. He needed ships, supplies, and sailors.

Columbus asked the queen of Spain for ships, supplies, and sailors.

HELP FROM A KING AND QUEEN

Columbus asked the kings of many countries for help. Everyone said no except King Ferdinand and Queen Isabel of Spain. They decided to help Columbus make his voyage. They gave him three ships: the Niña, the Pinta, and the Santa Maria. Columbus hired 90 sailors. In August, 1492, at the age of 41, Columbus set sail.

Columbus says good-bye to the queen before his first voyage.

LAND! LAND!

After 36 days of sailing, Columbus saw land. It was an island. It was in an area known today as the **Caribbean**. Columbus and his captains went ashore. Columbus claimed the new land for Spain. He was greeted by Native Americans living there. The Native Americans were friendly and helpful. Many helped Columbus find other islands. Columbus spent three months sailing around the Caribbean, exploring other islands.

Columbus claims land for Spain.

LAST VOYAGE

In the next 12 years, Columbus made three more voyages to the New World. On his last voyage, Columbus was **shipwrecked**. He had little food or fresh water. He became very ill. A year later, a ship arrived from Spain. At last, he was **rescued**.

When the ship arrived in Spain, Columbus was still very ill. A year and a half later, in 1506, Columbus died. He was 55 years old.

Columbus became ill in the New World.
He died in 1506 at the age of 55.

IMPORTANT DATES TO REMEMBER

1451	Born in Italy.
1465	Received his first job as a ship's boy.
1476	Sailed on many voyages learning to navigate a ship.
1480	Started seeking support for a voyage to prove the world was round.
1492	August, set sail with three ships. October, landed in the Caribbean.
1493	Spent years exploring the New World
1506	Died in Spain (May 20).

GLOSSARY

Caribbean (kar eh BEE un) — part of the Atlantic Ocean, east of Central America and north of South America

geography (jee AHG re fee) — the study of the Earth and its plant and animal life

navigate (NAV i gayt) — to steer a ship the way you want to go

rescued (RES kyood) — to save from danger

shipwrecked (SHIP rekt) — trapped away from home because of a ship that cannot sail

voyages (VOY ij EZ) — trips to places far away

INDEX

Further Reading

Carpenter, Eric. *Young Christopher Columbus: Discoverer of New Worlds.* Econo-Clad Books, 1999.
Dekay, James. *Meet Christopher Columbus.* Econo-Clad Books, 1999.
Gill, Jamie Spaht. *Christopher Columbus.* Aro Publishing, 1997.

Websites To Visit

www.encarta.msn.com
www.millersv.edu

About The Author

Trish Kline is a seasoned curriculum writer. She has written a great number of nonfiction books for the school and library market. Her print publishing credits include two dozen books as well as hundreds of newspaper and magazine articles, anthologies, short stories, poetry, and plays. She currently resides in Helena, Montana.